I0505611

Logistics
July 2015

ISBN-13: 978-1508866756
ISBN-10: 1508866759

Transoxiana@mail.com

Skype- strategicus7

Monthly journal of Logistics and Supply Chain Management Sector

Logistics, July 2015 Issue
ISBN-13: 978-1508866756   ISBN-10: 1508866759. To place free single page colored ad e mail us on Transoxiana@mail.com

GULF

BUSINESS JULY

2015

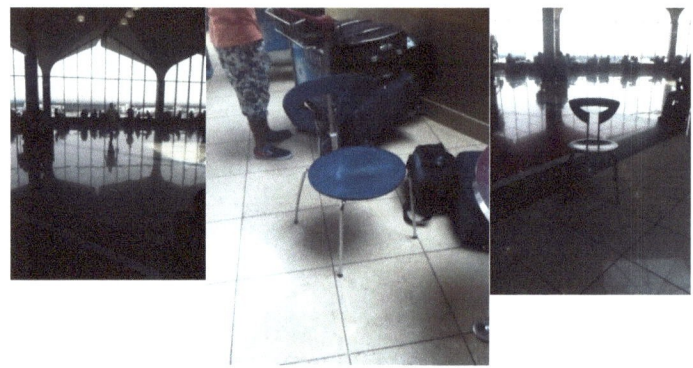

WHATS WRONG WITH DUBAI AIRPORT

WORLDS BEST INVESTMENT

Logistics, July 2015 Issue
ISBN-13: 978-1508866756   ISBN-10: 1508866759. To place free
single page colored ad e mail us on Transoxiana@mail.com

DAMAC PROPERTIES UAE

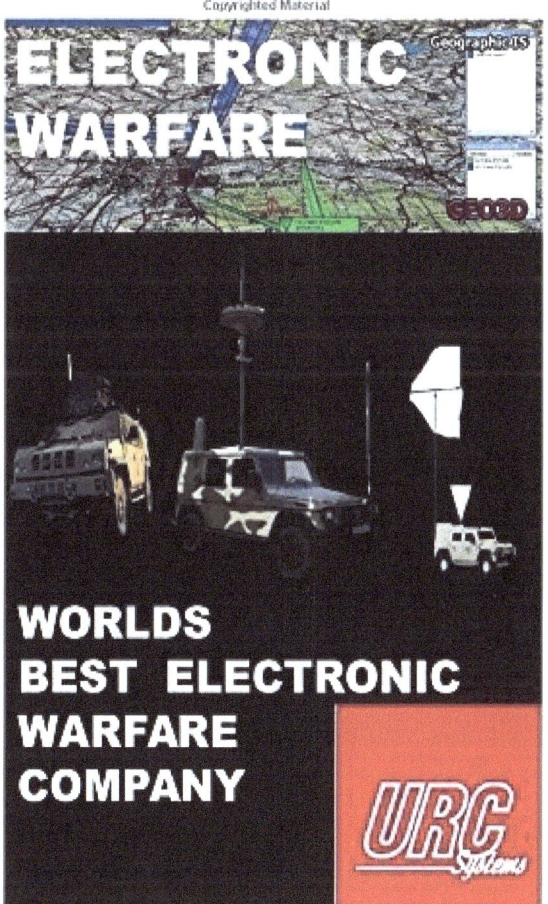

Logistics, July 2015 Issue

ISBN-13: 978-1508866756   ISBN-10: 1508866759. To place free single page colored ad e mail us on Transoxiana@mail.com

Risk Assessment, Security and Threat Perception Report, Pakistan

MARCH 2015

CSIO
CENTRE FOR STUDY OF INTELLIGENCE OPERATIONS

Logistics, July 2015 Issue

ISBN-13: 978-1508866756   ISBN-10: 1508866759. To place free single page colored ad e mail us on Transoxiana@mail.com

Logistics, July 2015 Issue

ISBN-13: 978-1508866756 ISBN-10: 1508866759. To place free
single page colored ad e mail us on Transoxiana@mail.com

Logistics, July 2015 Issue

ISBN-13: 978-1508866756   ISBN-10: 1508866759. To place free
single page colored ad e mail us on Transoxiana@mail.com

Logistics, July 2015 Issue
ISBN-13: 978-1508866756   ISBN-10: 1508866759. To place free
single page colored ad e mail us on Transoxiana@mail.com

Logistics, July 2015 Issue
ISBN-13: 978-1508866756 ISBN-10: 1508866759. To place free
single page colored ad e mail us on Transoxiana@mail.com

Logistics, July 2015 Issue

ISBN-13: 978-1508866756   ISBN-10: 1508866759. To place free single page colored ad e mail us on Transoxiana@mail.com

Logistics, July 2015 Issue
ISBN-13: 978-1508866756   ISBN-10: 1508866759. To place free single page colored ad e mail us on Transoxiana@mail.com

Logistics, July 2015 Issue
ISBN-13: 978-1508866756   ISBN-10: 1508866759. To place free single page colored ad e mail us on Transoxiana@mail.com

ANDERSON LLOYD
International Ltd

Date: 25ᵗ August 2010.

Ref: Authorised Representative for Anderson Lloyd International Ltd -Major Agha H Amin (Retired).

I am pleased to confirm that Anderson Lloyd International Ltd have secured the services in Afghanistan of Major Agha H Amin (Retired). The Major will have full rights to introduce clients to Anderson Lloyd International Ltd and we are very happy to have secured this arrangement.

I can confirm that the Major will be able to liaise between clients in Afghanistan and Anderson Lloyd International Ltd; the leading brokers for all classes of insurance in Afghanistan. Anderson Lloyd International Ltd deal with Lloyds of London as well as select American insurance companies to provide our clients with the right cover at the right price.

Anderson Lloyd International Ltd deals with some of the largest companies operating in Afghanistan and has an excellent reputation in the insurance market.

Lloyds of London have an excellent reputation and a long history and we have an excellent relationship with many Lloyds Brokers and Underwriting Syndicates.

I trust that this letter will assist you in dealing with the Major and I am happy to answer any questions that you may have.

Anderson Lloyd International Ltd has offices in Kuwait and the UK and has dealt in the insurance business for many years.

Best regards,

Michael J Ellery,

Director,

Anderson Lloyd International Ltd.

P.O. Box 679, Yarmouk, Kuwait, 72657
Courier Address : Office 7, Bldg. 3, Kuwait Free Trade Zone, Shuwaikh, Kuwait
Tel.: +965 4610081 · Fax : +965 4610085 E-mail: office@andersonlloydintl.com www.andersonlloydintl.com

Logistics, July 2015 Issue

ISBN-13: 978-1508866756   ISBN-10: 1508866759. To place free single page colored ad e mail us on Transoxiana@mail.com

Logistics, July 2015 Issue
ISBN-13: 978-1508866756   ISBN-10: 1508866759. To place free single page colored ad e mail us on Transoxiana@mail.com

Logistics, July 2015 Issue

ISBN-13: 978-1508866756   ISBN-10: 1508866759. To place free single page colored ad e mail us on Transoxiana@mail.com

Logistics, July 2015 Issue

ISBN-13: 978-1508866756   ISBN-10: 1508866759. To place free single page colored ad e mail us on Transoxiana@mail.com

TRANSOXIANA PROVIDES FUEL TRANSPORTATION SERVICES FROM KARACHI PORT AND PORT QASIM TO AFGHANISTAN.

Logistics, July 2015 Issue

ISBN-13: 978-1508866756   ISBN-10: 1508866759. To place free single page colored ad e mail us on Transoxiana@mail.com

TRANSOXIAN A LOGISTICS

TX

LOGISTICS

Logistics, July 2015 Issue
ISBN-13: 978-1508866756   ISBN-10: 1508866759. To place free
single page colored ad e mail us on Transoxiana@mail.com

Logistics, July 2015 Issue

ISBN-13: 978-1508866756   ISBN-10: 1508866759. To place free single page colored ad e mail us on Transoxiana@mail.com

TRANSPORTING FUEL TO KABUL VIA MAHIPAR DEFILE

Logistics, July 2015 Issue
ISBN-13: 978-1508866756   ISBN-10: 1508866759. To place free
single page colored ad e mail us on Transoxiana@mail.com

WITH LTC DAVID OSINSKI IN AFGHANISTAN

Logistics, July 2015 Issue

ISBN-13: 978-1508866756   ISBN-10: 1508866759. To place free single page colored ad e mail us on Transoxiana@mail.com

CHIEF TECHNICAL OFFICER OF TRANSOXIANA RECEIVES DIPLOMA OF ADVANCEV
MILITARY ENGINEERING AT US ARMY ENGINEER SCHOOL FORT BELVOIR VIRGINIA-1964

Lt Gen A.D Starbird DIRECTOR OF DEFENSE,COMMUNICATIONS
AGENCY PRESENTS DIPLOMA TO GRADUATING STUDENTS OF THE
3RD ECCC USAES ASSISTED BY Lt Col J.P Puff,US ARMY ENGINEER
SCHOOL FORT BELVOIR ,VIRGINIA 21 SEP 1964

Logistics, July 2015 Issue

ISBN-13: 978-1508866756   ISBN-10: 1508866759. To place free
single page colored ad e mail us on Transoxiana@mail.com

Logistics, July 2015 Issue

ISBN-13: 978-1508866756   ISBN-10: 1508866759. To place free single page colored ad e mail us on Transoxiana@mail.com

LPG TRANSPORT FROM TAJIKISTAN TO
AFGHANISTAN,CROSSING THE OXUS RIVER AT BANDAR SHER
KHAN

Logistics, July 2015 Issue

ISBN-13: 978-1508866756   ISBN-10: 1508866759. To place free
single page colored ad e mail us on Transoxiana@mail.com

Logistics, July 2015 Issue

ISBN-13: 978-1508866756   ISBN-10: 1508866759. To place free
single page colored ad e mail us on Transoxiana@mail.com

SNC·LAVALIN

SNC•LAVALIN Inc.
2525 Pitfield Blvd
Montreal, Quebec
Canada H4S 1W8

Telephone: (514) 334-8780, x9251
Fax: (514) 334-2610
Willy.Kotluga@snclavalinltd.com

April 28, 2009

To Whom It May Concern

Subject: Reference for Mr. Agha Humayun Amin, President of Afghan Toll

Dear Sir/Madam,

It is without any reservation that we give a high recommendation for the services that Mr. Agha Humayun Amin, President of Afghan Toll, provided to our company on the ADB funded CASA-1000 Project to do a feasibility study on bringing power from Kyrgyz Republic and Tajikistan through Afghanistan to Pakistan. Afghan provided these support services from November 2007 through September 2008.

Afghan Toll was our local consultant providing survey services to help us prepare the Environmental and Social Impact Assessments in Afghanistan for the 1000 MW High Voltage Direct Current (HVDC) line. Afghan Toll was responsible for collecting data and compiling the raw data, in addition to holding discussions with local residents. He also played a crucial role in suggesting confirming and in some places proposing modifications in the alignment of the initial proposed CASA 1000 transmission line based on ground confirmation factors of terrain and conflict with existing transmission lines.

Under very difficult circumstances, Afghan Toll collected the information from the Northern Afghanistan border with Tajikistan to Kabul and then to the Pakistan border near Peshawar. He did this in record time, exceeding our expectations, as he covered the entire route in person. The information that he provided was a key element in the assessments that have been forwarded to the World Bank, the Islamic Development Bank and the Asian Development Bank.

Although Afghan Toll is not specialized in Environment and Resettlement Impact Assessments, they were able provide all the information required by our specialists. We are very grateful for the services provided and would have no reservations in using their services on future work in Afghanistan.

Should you require additional information, it would be my pleasure to personally respond to your questions.

Best Regards,

Willy Kotluga

Willy Kotluga
Senior Director, Power Systems Consulting
Hydro and Power Systems

TRANSPORTING US ARMY HUMVEES FROM KARACHI TO AFGHANISTAN APRIL 2009

Logistics, July 2015 Issue
ISBN-13: 978-1508866756   ISBN-10: 1508866759. To place free single page colored ad e mail us on Transoxiana@mail.com

Logistics, July 2015 Issue
ISBN-13: 978-1508866756   ISBN-10: 1508866759. To place free
single page colored ad e mail us on Transoxiana@mail.com

KUNNAR OIL AND GAS FIELD WHERE WE LIFT LPG

Logistics, July 2015 Issue

ISBN-13: 978-1508866756   ISBN-10: 1508866759. To place free single page colored ad e mail us on Transoxiana@mail.com

**FUEL ON WAY FROM KARACHI TO
AFGHANISTAN**

Logistics, July 2015 Issue
ISBN-13: 978-1508866756   ISBN-10: 1508866759. To place free
single page colored ad e mail us on Transoxiana@mail.com

Logistics, July 2015 Issue

ISBN-13: 978-1508866756   ISBN-10: 1508866759. To place free single page colored ad e mail us on Transoxiana@mail.com

WE HAVE SUPPLIED FUEL IN MOST DANGEROUS PLACES IN THE WORLD LIKE WAZIRISTAN AND FATA

Logistics, July 2015 Issue

ISBN-13: 978-1508866756   ISBN-10: 1508866759. To place free single page colored ad e mail us on Transoxiana@mail.com

Logistics, July 2015 Issue

ISBN-13: 978-1508866756   ISBN-10: 1508866759. To place free
single page colored ad e mail us on Transoxiana@mail.com

Logistics, July 2015 Issue

ISBN-13: 978-1508866756   ISBN-10: 1508866759. To place free
single page colored ad e mail us on Transoxiana@mail.com

View from
TRANSOXIANA
Monitoring Post at Lataband
Pass 2008

Logistics, July 2015 Issue

ISBN-13: 978-1508866756   ISBN-10: 1508866759. To place free single page colored ad e mail us on Transoxiana@mail.com

Logistics, July 2015 Issue
ISBN-13: 978-1508866756 ISBN-10: 1508866759. To place free
single page colored ad e mail us on Transoxiana@mail.com

Burnt Oil tanker being inspected for Insurance
Report

Logistics, July 2015 Issue
ISBN-13: 978-1508866756   ISBN-10: 1508866759. To place free
single page colored ad e mail us on Transoxiana@mail.com

Logistics, July 2015 Issue

ISBN-13: 978-1508866756   ISBN-10: 1508866759. To place free single page colored ad e mail us on Transoxiana@mail.com

TARIFF RATE

1.   **SINGLE PAGE COLOURED AD – FREE**
2.   **MULTIPLE PAGE COLOURED AD- 100 USD PER PAGE**
3.   **FRONT COVER PLACEMENT ON TITLE PAGE- 1500 USD**

E MAIL ADDRESS TO PLACE AD –
Transoxiana@mail.com

Logistics, July 2015 Issue
ISBN-13: 978-1508866756   ISBN-10: 1508866759. To place free single page colored ad e mail us on Transoxiana@mail.com

www.ingramcontent.com/pod-product-compliance
Lightning Source LLC
Chambersburg PA
CBHW041144180526

45159CB00002BB/729